For my niece and nephews—B.G.

STERLING CHILDREN'S BOOKS
New York

An Imprint of Sterling Publishing Co., Inc.
1166 Avenue of the Americas
New York, NY 10036

ISBN 978-1-4549-3202-4

Distributed in Canada by Sterling Publishing Co., Inc.
c/o Canadian Manda Group, 664 Annette Street
Toronto, Ontario M6S 2C8, Canada
Distributed in the United Kingdom by GMC Distribution Services
Castle Place, 166 High Street, Lewes, East Sussex BN7 1XU, England
Distributed in Australia by NewSouth Books
45 Beach Street, Coogee, NSW 2034, Australia

For information about custom editions, special sales, and premium and corporate purchases, please
contact Sterling Special Sales at 800-805-5489 or specialsales@sterlingpublishing.com.

Manufactured in China

Lot #:
2 4 6 8 10 9 7 5 3 1
10/18

sterlingpublishing.com

PHOTOGRAPHS: Alamy: Sergey Novikov: 17; **Depositphotos:** © sernovik: 24;
Getty Images: Esbin-Anderson: 5 right; Library of Congress/corbis/VCG: 2 inset left; Tom & Dee McCarthy: 12;
Thomas Northcut: 23; **iStock:** 3DMAVR: 4 bottom; adventtr: 4 background; amriphoto: 5 left;
FatCamera: cover, 7, 13, 19; Christopher Futcher: 20; garymilner: 2 inset right; kali9: 14, 21;
monkeybusinessimages: 9 right; pepifoto: 4 top; pharut: 2 background; RBFried: 14, back cover top; Andre Rich: 1;
Library of Congress: 2 inset right; **Shutterstock.com:** Sergey Novikov: 9 left; Brad Sauter: 6;
Stocksy United: © Kelly Knox: 10; Tana Teel: back cover bottom; **SuperStock:** © marco albonico: 18;
ThinkStock: Stacy Barnett: 11; Fuse: 3

LET'S PLAY
BASKETBALL

By Bob Gurnett

Everything You Need to Know for Your First Practice

STERLING CHILDREN'S BOOKS
New York

History

In 1891, Dr. James Naismith put a peach basket on a post. Then, some of his college students played the very first game of basketball. The final score was only 1–0! The game of basketball has changed a lot since then. It's now one of the biggest sports in the world, played by famous athletes like Michael Jordan and LeBron James. Millions play basketball on playgrounds all over the world, as well as in youth leagues, high school, college, and professional leagues. Basketball owes its popularity to its simplicity. All you need to play a game is a hoop, a ball, and some friends.

GLOSSARY

Keep an eye out for these important basketball words!

Assist—A pass to a teammate that leads to a made basket.

Backboard—The glass or plastic behind the hoop.

Block—Stopping a shot in the air with your hand.

Box out—Positioning yourself in front of an opposing player for a rebound.

Dribble—Bouncing the ball off the ground. You must dribble to move with the ball.

Foul—Making illegal contact with someone, usually when they are shooting.

Free throw—A shot taken from the free throw line with no one defending. Worth one point.

Jump shot—Standard basketball shot. Jump and shoot.

Layup—A shot very close to the basket, usually by bouncing the ball off the backboard.

Pass—Throwing the ball to a teammate.

Pivot foot—The foot a player plants and cannot move when they have the ball and have stopped dribbling.

Rebound—Grabbing the ball after a missed shot.

Steal—Taking the ball from an opposing player.

Travel—Moving the ball without dribbling.

The Gear

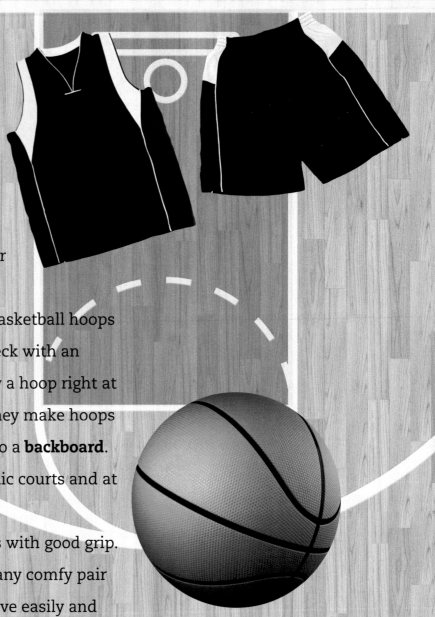

You only need two things to play basketball: a ball and a hoop. You can dribble and shoot baskets alone, but it is more fun with friends.

Basketballs come in different sizes, but a parent can help you pick the right one for your age. Make sure the ball is inflated (ask an adult for help) so you can get a good bounce from it.

Once you've got a ball, you just need a hoop. Basketball hoops can be found in most playgrounds and parks. Check with an adult to see where you can play. There is probably a hoop right at your school! A standard hoop is 10 feet tall, but they make hoops that are 8 feet tall for kids. The hoop is attached to a **backboard**. You can find these basketball hoops at some public courts and at most elementary schools.

The only other essential gear is a pair of shoes with good grip. Some kids will have flashy basketball shoes, but any comfy pair of sneakers will work. Just make sure you can move easily and get good traction when running. Lace them up tight!

Offense

Basketball seems simple at first: score a basket for two points, a three-pointer for three points, or a **free throw** for one point. Score more points than the other team and you win! But how you score those points (and how you keep the other team from scoring) is where the game gets complicated! Let's start by talking about how to score on offense.

Dribbling

If you want to move with the ball, you must **dribble**. Dribbling is repeatedly bouncing the ball with one hand. It is the only way to move the ball by yourself. If you don't dribble, it is a **travel**, which is against the rules. If you travel, the ref will blow the whistle, and the other team will get the ball.

HOW TO DRIBBLE:

1. Bounce the ball with your fingertips. Don't use the palm of your hand. Let your fingertips control the ball.

2. Use your wrist, not your whole arm, to push the ball down.

3. Don't pick up the ball.

4. Keep the ball low—about waist high or lower. Your dribble should be quick and steady.

5. Keep your knees bent, but your back straight, to maintain good balance.

6. Keep your head up! If you're looking at the ball you can't see your teammates, defenders, or the basket.

7. Use your other arm to shield the ball from defenders.

DRIBBLING TIPS:

- Learn to dribble with both hands so you can switch if a defender tries to steal the ball.

- You can practice dribbling anywhere! You don't need a hoop. Just don't do it in inside your home!

- If you stop dribbling, you can only move one foot. The other has to remain planted. That is your **pivot** foot.

Passing

There are five players on a team. It is important to work together to score. **Passing** is a great way to get your other teammates involved and increase your chance to score. If you make a pass that helps a teammate score, that is called an **assist**.

There are three types of basic passes:
Chest pass—This pass starts at your chest. Use both hands to throw the ball to another teammate. Make sure they can catch it at chest level!

Bounce pass—Throw this pass like a chest pass, but bounce it off the ground. If you do it right, it'll bounce high enough for a teammate to catch it.

Overhead pass—Hold the ball above your head with both hands. Your thumbs should be behind the ball. This is great when passing over a defender!

PASSING TIPS:

- Don't be afraid to pass. Passing is not just for when you can't shoot. If you see a teammate with an even better shot than yours, pass it to them!

- Make sure to throw passes a teammate can easily catch.

- Step toward the person you are targeting when throwing a pass.

- If you are catching a pass, step toward the pass while it is in the air.

- Passing is what makes five separate basketball players into a team. It is important to get everyone involved. If a teammate hasn't touched the ball in a while, pass it to them! Share the ball and share the energy!

Shooting

You now know how to move the ball, but how do you score? You score by shooting the ball! If you get the ball through the hoop, it is worth points. The team with the most points at the end of the game wins! Let's go over the different ways to get the ball in the hoop.

JUMP SHOT

The **jump shot** is your long-range weapon. Use this to hit mid-range and long shots. The jump shot can be worth either two or three points, depending on how far away from the basket you shoot the ball. A jump shot earns three points when it's made from a long distance. For now, you will want to focus on perfecting your two-point jump shot and save the three-pointers for when you're older and taller.

HOW TO SHOOT A BASIC JUMP SHOT:

1. Spot up. In other words, get to where you want to shoot by dribbling or getting a pass.

2. Get your feet shoulder width apart and bend your knees.

3. Bring the ball up toward your head, resting the ball in your shooting hand and using your off hand (the hand you're not shooting with) to steady it.

4. Now jump! Always jump straight up. Don't go off to the side. Use your momentum to launch the ball toward the hoop! A good jump shot always has a high arc.

5. Follow through so your ball gets backspin.

6. Practice makes perfect. It may take a while to get the arm strength to shoot a jump shot. Start off by shooting close to the hoop. As you get stronger, shoot from farther away.

LAYUP

The **layup** is the most basic shot, and it is worth two points if the ball goes in. If you have a clear path to the basket, this is the shot you take.

HOW TO DO A LAYUP:

1. Dribble up toward the basket.

2. Gather the ball two steps before you are going to jump.

3. If you are on the right side of the basket, use your right hand and jump off your left foot.

4. If you are on the left side of the basket, use your left hand and jump off your right foot.

5. Get as high as you can, stretch out, and lightly bounce the ball off the square on the backboard and the ball should fall into the hoop.

LAYUP TIPS:

• Always make sure you are jumping off the opposite foot. If you are doing a right-handed layup, jump off your left foot. If you're left-handed, jump off your right.

• Practice shooting layups with both your left and right hands. It can be tricky, but once you get the hang of it, it is very useful.

• Soft hands! You don't need to throw the ball at the backboard. Just let it hit as softly as you can and it will fall into the hoop.

FREE THROWS

If you are fouled, you may get a trip to the **free throw** line. You will get to shoot without anyone guarding you. A made free throw is worth 1 point.

HOW TO MAKE A FREE THROW:

1. Take your time. No one is guarding you.

2. Repetition is key. Try to shoot free throws the same way every time.

3. You don't have to jump if you don't want to. Shoot however is most comfortable.

4. Plant your feet and bend your knees.

5. Keep your eyes on the basket.

6. Follow through!

Defense

If your team doesn't have the ball, it is your job to keep the other team from scoring. That is called defense. Defense isn't just played when the player in front of you has the ball. You should always be playing defense! If you are guarding the ball handler, you are playing on-ball defense, but if you aren't, you still need to play off-ball defense. But no matter who you are defending, it all comes down to having a strong defensive stance.

HOW TO GET INTO A DEFENSIVE STANCE:

1. Keep your feet wide! This will help you move quickly and keep your balance.

2. Get low! You won't lose your balance and you can move quickly.

3. Try to stand on the front of your feet with less weight on your heels so you can move and react fast.

4. Keep your head up! Don't watch the ball. Instead, watch the other player's chest or waist so you can know what direction they are going.

ON-BALL DEFENSE

If the player you are defending has the ball, you want to keep in between your player and the hoop. Here on some tips for on-ball defense:

1. Keep your head up! Don't get lost looking at the ball or the ground.
2. Keep your balance! Stay low and wide. If you lose your balance, they will blow by you.
3. Keep your hands up! Active hands can help stop the ball and make shots more difficult.
4. If the player goes for a shot, try to get your hand on the ball. If you stop the shot, it is called a **block**.
5. Try to go for the ball and slap it away while they dribble. If you can get it away from them, it is a **steal**.
6. Be careful not to **foul**. Don't hit anything but the ball. If you hit the player, it is a foul. They may get free throws.

OFF-BALL DEFENSE

What if the person you are defending doesn't have the ball? You still must defend! Here are some tips for off-ball defense:

1. Try to stay between the ball and the player you are defending. If the player can't get a pass, they can't score.
2. Help other players if the defender gets beat. Sometimes your teammate will lose their balance or just get dribbled past. It is up to the rest of the team to help!
3. Talk! The team should always be talking so they know what is going on. Your coach will teach you what to say in certain situations.

The most important part of defense is to keep the other team away from the hoop, and to prevent them from scoring. Your job is to stop the ball! If you are between the ball and the hoop, it is much harder for them to score.

Rebounding

If you play good defense, the opposing team might miss their shot! The ball will bounce off the rim, the backboard, or miss the mark completely, and it is anyone's ball! If you are able to grab the ball, that is a **rebound**. Rebounds are huge because they keep the other team from getting another shot or give your team an extra one. Every player on the team should be working and hustling for rebounds. You can get a rebound on defense or offense. If your team misses a shot on offense, you can get the rebound and still score.

The most important thing to do when rebounding is to **box out** the other team. A box out is getting in between another player and the ball. You then use your body to keep them from getting to the ball before you or your teammate.

HOW TO BOX OUT:

1. Get low! Bend your knees for great balance.

2. Put your back to your opponent.

3. Spread your arms out to your sides. Try to predict where the ball will go if the shot is missed.

4. If you have the right position, the other player cannot get to the ball without fouling you!

If you and your team all box out the opposing players, you should be clear to grab the rebound. Talk to each other and try to time your jump to grab the ball. It takes practice but if you do it right, you'll be really helping your team!

Who Is on the Court?

Basketball has 3 basic positions: guard, forward, and center. Which position will you play? Trick question: you'll play all of them! To be a good basketball player, you should try to play every position. Each uses skills that are essential to master basketball.

GUARD

Guards are the primary ball handlers. They bring the ball up the court and will pass the ball to teammates. Their job is to get everyone involved in the offense with passing and drives to the hoop. Guards will normally play a little farther from the basket and shoot longer shots, but a good guard is still effective under the hoop.

FORWARD

A forward will always be trying to get closer to the hoop. Their job is to get as close as they can for layups and short shots, but a very good forward can still hit long shots. They also are the primary rebounders, boxing out opponents to get the ball before the other team.

CENTER

A center is meant to play close to the hoop. They use their strength to get into the best position possible before they are passed the ball. A good center can have a soft touch around the rim but also pull down tons of rebounds. The best centers can also hit a jump shot against other centers farther from the rim.

Don't worry about what position you will play. Players will be able to play every position and use all the skills. If you spent a lot of time in your last game working on guard skills, mix it up and ask your coach to teach you some under the hoop, center moves.

Practice

Your first practice! Remember, your coach is in charge. What they say goes! They will make you run drills, play scrimmages, and practice plays together.

Drills are used to practice skills—like shooting, rebounding, and dribbling—when the game isn't on. Drills can be as simple as dribbling around cones or passing to your teammates. Your coach will have some drills for you to improve your fundamentals!

Scrimmage is when you split into teams and play other kids on your team to practice. Coach may have you play 2 on 2, 3 on 3, or even the same size as a game with 5 on 5. These scrimmages help you use those skills you learned in the drills.

Tips for Game Day!

1. Game day is here! Get to the court when the coach said. If you are late, you might not get to play.

2. Pay attention to the referees. They will be in black and white stripes. Their job is to make sure everyone follows the rules and has fun. They are in charge, so always listen to them.

3. Stay hydrated throughout the game. Drink plenty of water!

4. Even if you aren't in the game, pay attention! You can learn a lot by watching others play. Maybe you see a kid who is a great shooter on the other team. If you have to go defend him, you will know to play extra tough defense.

5. If you are not playing in the game, be sure to cheer on your teammates.

6. Be a good sport. Don't get too frustrated or mad. If you feel yourself getting mad or upset, tell your coach and take a break. Basketball is supposed to be fun!

7. At the end of the game, shake hands and say "good game" to players from both teams, win or lose!

What Else Can You Do to Improve?

- Dribble all the time. Dribble in the driveway, on the sidewalk, walking to school, walking the dog! Dribble for 20 seconds with your right hand, then switch to your left hand for 20 seconds. See how long you can go!

- Practice shooting at the park or at home.

- Do 100 layups. Remember, if you shoot the layup with your right hand, jump off your left foot. Now try it with your left hand and jump off your right foot.

- See how many free throws you can shoot in a row without missing.

Every basketball player had their first practice. Even NBA players were once beginners, just like you. Now let's play basketball!

A Note to Your Biggest Fan

Parents and caregivers can play a key role in helping kids who are stepping onto the hardwood for the first time.

Model model behavior. Teamwork and sportsmanship are critical to any game. Provide encouragement and support to your child, to your child's team, and to your child's opponents. Show respect to the coach and other volunteers.

Let the coach coach. You have a couple of jobs to do, but coaching isn't one of them. Be sure your child is on time and ready to play, then take a seat and take it easy.

Away from the court, ask the coach to provide practice tips that will support the team methods and message, and privately discuss any concerns you have about your child's playing time or performance.

Temper your temper. As any professional player will tell you, missing a big shot, turning the ball over, and losing are all part of the game. Missteps and missed calls can be frustrating for everybody. Keep cool! The point of basketball at this level is for your child to develop new skills, be active, play with friends, and have fun. Learning to take mistakes in stride will help your child become a happier, more confident player.